Evolving Understanding
An Ordinary Feminist's Reflections
on the Teachings of Christ

Copyright © 2017 Mountain Cat Media LLC.
All Rights Reserved

Published in the United States
by Mountain Cat Media LLC

ISBN-13: 978-0-692-81945-6

Printed in the United States

The Scripture quotations contained herein are from the New Revised Standard Version Bible, copyright ©1989 Division of Christian Education of the National Council of Churches of Christ in the U.S.A. Used by permission. All rights reserved.

Cover photo by Sergey Nivens
Licensed through Adobe Systems Inc.
Cover design by Sandra Greenberg

No part of this document or may be reproduced or transmitted in any form, by any means (electronic, photocopying, recording, or otherwise) without the prior written permission of the publisher.

MOUNTAIN CAT MEDIA LLC
P.O. Box 74
Bridgeton, MO 63044
www.mountaincatmedia.com

*This book is dedicated to my parents,
who showed by example what
quiet, steadfast faith truly is.*

Table of Contents

Introduction: An Ordinary Feminist

1

Chapter 1: The Nature of God

6

Chapter 2: Gospel Perspective

24

Chapter 3: Who Are The Inheritors?

32

Chapter 4: Mary, the Mother of Jesus

46

Chapter 5: Belief and Disbelief

61

Chapter 6: Heroism, or Rather, Heroine-ism

69

Chapter 7: The Gospel of Mary Magdalen

86

Chapter 8: Marriage, Divorce and Adultery

98

Chapter 9: Was Jesus Married?

111

Chapter 10: The Role of Women In Ministry

117

Introduction:
An Ordinary Feminist

If you think "Ordinary Feminist" is an odd term, it may be because when I Googled feminism, I found a lot of versions: liberal, radical, Third Wave, socialist, eco, feminazi - the list goes on, and "Ordinary" is not included. So, what, you may ask, is an ordinary feminist? That would be me. I came up with the term because none of the others fit. There is no sub-text to my feminism. I believe in the original definition of feminism: men and women are equal, period. I don't think either gender is meant to be subservient or superior to the other; that two people with the same skills, experience, and background should be offered the same salary for the same job; and that both men and women have the ability to be nurturing, stay-at-home parents. Women and men alike should be allowed to choose their paths in life, to work inside or outside the home as fits their circumstances, beliefs, and interests, without worrying about being frowned upon by those who make different choices. My daughter calls herself an "equalist," and I like that term, too. The kind of feminism I believe in really is just that, everyone is equal. I suppose my preferred use of the term feminist could be generational. I also consider myself a reasonably ordinary woman, hence I am an Ordinary Feminist.

I am also a Christian, and I don't see Christianity contradicting my feminism. In fact, I think the teachings of Christ support a view of gender equality. There are those at the far fringes of the spectrum, whether fundamentalist Christian or radically feminist, who feel Christianity and feminism are incompatible. But I see the teachings of Christ as refreshingly egalitarian in nature, especially considering the society of Christ's day.

I should warn you, if you are looking for a high scholarly work by a professor of philosophy or some such, this isn't it. However, if you like friendly discussions of philosophy and theology, then please keep reading. No one should ever feel discouraged to discuss these subjects just because they don't have a degree in it. Intelligent and fascinating discussions of both can come from any education level or walk of life. For the record, I'm a mostly self-taught freelance writer and lyricist with a couple of years of college gathered sporadically. I've worn many additional hats over the years, which I honestly think describes most women.

As I sit in church, I often think about the readings and sermons and have had lovely discussions in my head about different aspects and interpretations of what was said. Unfortunately, my schedule usually doesn't allow me the luxury of attending discussion groups or taking theology classes. Combine these things with the writer side of me constantly saying "you should write this down," and you have the impetus for this book. The subtitle came to me in church one Sunday morning in one of those "ah-ha" moments a writer gets when musing inspiration gels and becomes words on paper. Was this God nudging me? I'd like to think so, but I certainly don't claim any obvious divine intervention. Every writer will tell you never look the gift horse of inspiration in the mouth.

This book is generously laced with bible passages (I use the New Revised Standard Version). While I love the idea readers might be inspired to read the bible, I don't want you to have to constantly jump from this book to looking things up. So passages I discuss are, for the most part, right there in the chapter.

My wish for this book is to have it spark conversations someplace other than in my own head. It is not a scholarly treatise with all kinds of ancient reference material. For probably 90% of it, it is just the bible I discuss. It is a dialogue for those like me, ordinary people living ordinary lives, who are exploring their faith and seeking to balance their feminist ideals with their Christianity. I hope you enjoy it.

Chapter 1
The Nature of God

One of the arguments some feminists have with more traditional-minded Christians is the question of whether God is male or female. Some feminists insist on calling God she, causing the traditional-minded Christian to insist God is a he. It may be a cliché, but I think William Shakespeare actually said it best in Romeo and Juliet, when Juliet proclaims: "That which we call a rose, by any other name, would smell as sweet." God, by whatever name or pronoun, is still God.

I believe everyone who accepts the existence of a supreme being as Creator of the universe, is worshiping and revering the *same* Creator regardless of name or chosen way to worship. Might not such a Creator reach out to each human culture in a way each culture would best relate?

The 90's science fiction show *Babylon 5* had two great episodes regarding human religion. In season one's *Parliament of Dreams*, the commander is supposed to give a "demonstration of Earth's dominant belief system" to representatives of several races. The commander finally takes the participants down a very long line of people, introducing them to a representative of every Earth religion. In season three's *Convictions*, monks come to the station and take up residence to learn all the different names of God, including the names alien races use. This is not just science fiction. In an unmeasurable universe, there is a strong probability of other planets with civilizations on them. They were also created by God, and we can only imagine what might be their name for God and their way of worshiping.

Our own world has many belief systems. Christianity is what I personally believe, and so it's right for me. I would not presume to tell someone else it is the only "right" one and thus they must follow it, too.

This is because I see spirituality as a gift from God. Whereas I see religion as a human construct. In Genesis, when the universe is created, no mention is made of creating religion. There are no rabbis, no priests, no doctrine or dogma, no ceremonies, etc., just a personal relationship between creator and creation. Humans invented religion in an attempt to understand the unfathomable. God communicated with us and we interpreted as best we could. But it was still *our* interpretation of something we struggle to understand. Leaders, ceremonies, and organizations were developed by us to make us comfortable. God does not need religion, we do.

I call God, Father, and generally use the pronoun He. This is not because I am convinced

God is male. It is for my own convenience, a way for my limited brain to grasp the incomprehensible. I do not need to believe God is one gender or another to believe God exists and is the creator of the universe.

In fact, I don't believe God has any gender. God is just God. God is everywhere and everything all at the same time. Why would a being – omnipotent, omnipresent, and limitless, for whom nothing is impossible – need to have the limiting parameters of a gender? As humans, we can never hope to fully understand the true nature and essence of God, so we use convenient terms of comfort. Jesus himself calls God spirit.

John 4:24:
24 "God is spirit, and those who worship him must worship in spirit and truth."

In Jesus's time, a lot of the known civilized societies, including Israel, were patriarchal. If Israel had been matriarchal, with women making the rules, God might have been depicted differently. Father was head of house, protector of the family, and guide to the young. Father is a comforting name. Mother, which some feminists use, is also a comforting name, one of nurture, wisdom and care. Jesus as brother, a child of God like us, brings to full the comfort of family. What all of these terms have in common is they make people feel a sense of love and belonging. Human terms for human comfort.

    In Christianity, God is depicted by three aspects: God the Father, God the Son, and God the Holy Spirit. This Trinity is described as one being in three parts. In itself, it is a difficult concept. I picture a being of pure light and energy which can split a part of itself off, send it elsewhere, then bring the part back to join with the whole. The part split off is as much the being as the part which remains, even if the split off part enters a human woman and joins itself with her egg to form a baby. At his Ascension, I see this part of God who became the human, Jesus, shedding this human form and rejoined with its non-corporeal self.

Acts 1:9

9 When he had said this, as they were watching, he was lifted up, and a cloud took him out of their sight.

Could it be only his non-corporeal spirit is what they saw go up? That the human shell was left behind to be buried? Why not?

Within this Trinity, God the Father and God the Son are depicted in the bible as male, while God as Holy Spirit is most often depicted in a gender neutral manner. Consider Paul's letter to the Romans explaining the Spirit.

Romans 8:1-6

There is therefore now no condemnation for those who are in Christ Jesus. 2 For the law of the Spirit of life in Christ Jesus has set you free from the law of sin and of death. 3 For God has done what the law, weakened by flesh, could not do: by sending his own Son in the likeness of sinful flesh, and to deal with sin, he condemned sin in the flesh, 4 so that the just requirement of the law might be fulfilled in us, who walk not according to the flesh but according to the Spirit. 5 For those who live according to the flesh set their minds on the things of the flesh, but those who live according to the Spirit set their minds on the things of the Spirit. 6 To set the mind on the flesh is death, but to set the mind on the Spirit is life and peace.

The Holy Spirit is usually depicted as gentle, nurturing, and comforting, traits often associated with women. The workings of the Holy Spirit are often coupled with imparting knowledge and wisdom. The Spirit of Wisdom is definitely referred to as feminine. In the Old Testament, feminine Wisdom is described as being first in creation, having been brought into being before the universe, or anything earthly, was created. Described here in the Proverbs of Solomon, the son of King David:

Proverbs 8:1-5 and 22-32

1 Does not wisdom call, and does not understanding raise her voice?

2 On the heights, beside the way, at the crossroads she takes her stand;

3 beside the gates in front of the town, at the entrance of the portals, she calls out:

4 "To you, O people, I call, and my cry is to all that live.

5 O simple ones, learn prudence; acquire intelligence, you who lack it.

22 "The Lord created me at the beginning of his work, the first of his acts of long ago. 23 Ages ago I was set up, at the first, before the beginning of the earth. 24 When there were no depths I was brought forth, when there were no springs abounding with water. 25 Before the mountains had been shaped, before the hills, I was brought forth –

26 when he had not yet made earth and fields, or the world's first bits of soil. 27 When he established the heavens, I was there, when he drew a circle on the face of the deep, 28 when he made firm the skies above, when he established the fountains of the deep, 29 when he assigned to the sea its limit, so that the waters might not transgress his command, when he marked out the foundations of the earth, 30 then I was beside him, like a master worker; and I was daily his delight, rejoicing before him always, 31 rejoicing in his inhabited world and delighting in the human race, 32 and now my children listen to me; happy are those who keep my ways.

Luke 7:35
35 "Nevertheless, wisdom is vindicated by all her children."

Matthew 11:19
(Last line of) 19 "Yet wisdom is vindicated by her deeds."

And of note above: there is no distinction made between men and women, but all people are told to "acquire intelligence" if they are lacking in it.

Now wisdom, telling us she was created by God, is not the Holy Spirit who is a part of God. However, it is easy to see how the Holy Spirit can be seen as the feminine aspect of God. The Holy Spirit is often mentioned as sending wisdom and knowledge when needed.

Luke 12:11-12

11 When they bring you before the synagogues, the rulers and the authorities, do not worry about how you are to defend yourselves or what you are to say; 12 for the Holy Spirit will teach you at that very hour what you ought to say."

To me, passages like this and others to be discussed, make it clear the bible shows the role of women, and of the feminine side of humanity, as important. The feminine aspect of our species is half of the whole of what it means to be human. To become human, Jesus had to be born and, since for humans, only women can give birth, a woman did have to be involved in the process.

At this point I should probably tell you something else about me: I don't view the bible as something God intended, in its entirety, to be taken with absolute literalness. Genesis describes mankind as being created in God's image, but does not say which image of God mankind is created in. Just like I do not see God as needing a gender, neither do I think our Creator has any need for a body except when he chooses to have one for our benefit. Genesis could also mean mankind was created in the image of God's intellect, or his spiritual image, or his moral image. It does not necessarily have to mean God's physical image. A corporeal body is limiting and God is limitless.

The wonderful thing about the bible is it is able to change, without actually changing, and so it evolves along side our understanding. The inspired word of God, not God being quoted verbatim. Some of it was written four to six thousand years ago, yet in such a way that the understanding and interpretation of its teachings could evolve along with the society who reads it. Now there's a miracle for you! Even Jesus tells his disciples that He can't teach them everything because they would not understand.

John 16:12
12 I still have many things to say to you, but you cannot bear them now.

Based on the bible, we once jailed scientists for saying the Earth is not the undeniable center of the universe. Look at poor Galileo in front of the Inquisition in the early seventeenth century. (Copernicus only avoided it by dying before they could charge him.) Thankfully, our understanding of God's vast creation has evolved and expanded, and the interpretation of the bible's teachings has evolved with our understanding. We stopped seeing scientific discovery as a threat to belief. We have medical science to cure or treat ailments which were once seen as demonic possession; we understand Earth is a tiny, insignificant (to the cosmos) planet which is part of a universe too big to measure; and we have walked on the moon. So many things which today we understand and take as common place, would have been incomprehensible to the people of Jesus' time. And on the cosmic scale of things, that's been the blink of an eye.

When my two adult children were young and asked about God creating the world, I told them yes,

God did create the world. I then said God used the Big Bang and evolution as the tools of creation. I see no contradiction between creationism and evolution. In fact, I think the passage "Let the waters bring forth swarms of living creatures" could be seen as a reference to evolution - microbial life teeming in the water, evolving and eventually leaving it. I see God as creating many wonderful tools to use in the creation of the world, and one of those was evolution. It is a self-replicating tool he continues to use, built–in to all he created, allowing not only our bodies, but our minds, our intellect, and thus our understanding, to also evolve.

Tim Griffin of Griffin Education Solutions (www.griffined.org) has a wonderful song called *God Made Evolution, Too*. You can listen to it on his website; the album is called *Over The Edge*. Brilliantly put, I couldn't have said it better.

I find it interesting there are two separate accounts of creation in Genesis, and both point to men and women being equal. In the account in Genesis 1, the creation of Adam and Eve is described this way:

> *Genesis 1: 26-28*
>
> *26Then God said, "Let us make humankind in our image, according to our likeness; and let them have dominion over the fish of the sea, and over the birds of the air, and over the cattle, and over all the wild animals of the earth, and over every creeping thing that creeps upon the earth." 27So God created humankind in his image, in the image of God he created them; male and female he created them. 28God blessed them, and God said to them "Be fruitful and multiply, and fill the earth and subdue it; and have dominion over the fish of the sea and over the birds of the air and over every living thing that moves upon the earth."*

The plural pronoun of "us" is interesting here. In Christian tradition, this reference is believed to mean the Holy Trinity of Father, Son, and Spirit. In Jewish tradition, it is thought to mean God referring to himself and the angels. Do you notice something else in this first version? Not one mention is made of the tree of the knowledge of good and evil.

Then, a different version is given. I wonder to what purpose? The second creation story lacks any mention of a timetable. The middle of verse four even says "In the day that the Lord God made the earth and the heavens." This version sounds like it was all done in one "day" and has a lot more geography in it, with the names of rivers given. One similarity is neither version says woman was created to be anything but man's equal.

Genesis 2:18

18Then the Lord God said, "It is not good that the man should be alone; I will make him a helper as his partner."

Helper. Partner. Not servant, not slave, not subject. Creation is given to "them," not only to Adam. No mention is made of either human having dominion over the other. The only dominion mentioned in either version is on humans having it over the rest of creation.

I look at the creation story in Genesis as a symbolic teaching tool, an extremely simplified story of the beginnings of Israel. At its core, it is the story of humanity being given the gifts of a beautiful world and of free will, and of making our first wrong choice with that free will.

God is the ultimate unanswerable question. The unknown we cannot hope to ever understand, representing all which is completely beyond our control. Seeing things as beyond our control is scary. As a whole, humans generally like their lives and world to be organized and predictable. We don't accept the fact that most of it is quite beyond our subjugation and instead come up with all kinds of ways to fool ourselves with the illusion of being in control. Take the weather. We can't control the weather but we can predict it. Even though we are not always right, those predictions give us a greater sense of stability. And if technology allows, you can bet we will attempt to control it in the future, erecting boundaries and perimeters around it. It's human nature.

But God is infinite, we cannot ever hope to control God, and yet we try. We give God boundaries, create a mental box for God to inhabit, where we can pull him out when we need him but not open the box when we're doing something God wouldn't like, and delude ourselves into thinking we're somehow in control.

When we believed the Earth was flat and the center of the universe, with all the heavens rotating around it, we felt important. Everything revolved around *us*. And God was depicted in art as an elderly, white grandfather figure. The idea of Manifest Destiny, and the arrogant belief of white, Christian Europeans as superior beings to the Native people of North America, is an extreme example of putting God in a controllable box to point to and say we know what God wants.

Humanity has a talent for being wrong about such things. We now know scientifically the Earth is not even the center of our galaxy, much less the universe. It can be very humbling to stand in a dark field and look up at the vastness of planets and stars and realize just how small and insignificant we are in comparison. Collectively, humanity has not been very good at being humble. History shows that as a whole arrogance comes much easier to us.

God created the universe, our world, and all creatures in it. Then humanity created religion to try to understand God. Some determined God must be male because they were male and felt superior because of it. Gender, as a box to put God in, is still a box.

But God doesn't stay in our boxes. He never has and never will. God cannot be contained by human methods, limited by human gender. The box of gender distinction is only our illusion, God doesn't need it.

God is always there when we need God. He's also always there when we think we don't need him or are doing something we shouldn't. We should never assume he'll stay in the boxes we construct. One thing I'm sure of – boxed is not part of God's nature.

Chapter 2
A Brief Look at Gospel Perspective

    If four people witness the same car accident, the police will have four different descriptions of what happened. All may describe what they saw and heard, but their perspectives and points of view are distinctive. Maybe they were on opposite corners of the intersection, or looking different directions, or considered parts of the accident - say the rain or speed of the car - to be more or less important. They also see through the particular lenses of their life experiences, for instance their own close calls at that very intersection.

The same can be said of history. Each country will teach the same dates and places where battles occurred, but how well or poorly the battle was waged and who was in the right, is all a matter of perspective. Just as the American Western expansion is viewed through a far less heroic lens by the Native Americans who were displaced by the European invaders. Today's animosity between Israel and the Palestinians, where each calls the other the aggressor, is because they each view the difficulties from a different perspective.

I see the gospels as Christ's teachings from four points of view, four ideas of what's important. All give their version of events, with each concentrating on different aspects of Christ's teachings filtered through individual perspectives.

We will never know definitively who wrote them. The prevailing hypophysis accepted by most scholars, however, is that Mark is the oldest gospel, that Matthew and Luke use Mark as part of their source material; that the author of John was one of the original disciples while Mark and Luke were not, that all were oral traditions first, and they were written between 68 and 110 C.E.

Two of the gospels describe Christ's birth, the other two barely mention it. Only in Luke does Pilot send Jesus to Harod. All mention two criminals crucified beside Jesus, yet only Luke depicts one of them as repentant and defending Jesus to the other. All show the religious establishment as testing Jesus and seeking to trap him. Yet John depicts, though briefly, the high priest Caiaphas as a sympathetic character who prophesies Jesus will die for the nation.

John 11:49-52

49 But one of them, Caiaphas, who was high priest that year, said to them, "You know nothing at all! 50 You do not understand that it is better for you to have one man die for the people then to have the whole nation destroyed." 51 He did not say this on his own, but being high priest that year he prophesied that Jesus was about to die for the nation, 52 and not for the nation only, but to gather into one the dispersed children of God.

This passage makes me wonder: what if the High Priests were actually trying to save people by sacrificing Jesus? Historical references to Pilate paint a much harsher picture of this minor governor then the biblical passages which make him a semi-sympathetic victim of circumstance. Roman governors tended to put insurrections down by violent means. Whole villages were wiped out as examples if they thought rebellion was being incited. By handing over the leader of what could have been seen by Rome as an insurrection, Caiaphas may have been trying to mitigate the damage and keep the greater number alive. The priests did not see themselves or their actions as evil. Perspective, again.

In Matthew, Jesus feeds five thousand with five loaves and two fish and ends up with twelve baskets of leftovers. In Mark, Jesus feeds four thousand with seven loaves and "a few small fish" and ends up with seven baskets of leftovers. The same incident from two perspectives? Or were these two different instances of the same miracle being performed? Whichever version, a miracle occurred which allowed an extremely large crowd to be fed when the resources on hand were severely limited.

The New Testament was not written until decades after Christ's life. Persecution was rampant and oral traditions among the lower classes were common practice. By the time each perspective was written, the stories had been repeated and taught for more than a generation.

Consistent through all the gospel perspectives is that Jesus saw women as having more value than it seemed the men of the time did, including the religious authorities. The women who followed Jesus were apostles and disciples as much as the twelve chosen. According to the dictionary, the definition of an apostle is: "any of the early followers of Jesus who carried the Christian message into the world." And the definition of a disciple is, in addition to the twelve: "any other professed follower of Christ in His lifetime." The women listened, learned, and faithfully followed Jesus the same as the men, and in many ways were more steadfast than the male disciples, even the chosen twelve.

The historical accuracy can be argued for and against in other books. For the purpose of this book, assume my acceptance of the bible as the inspired Word of God. Not always literal, especially the Old Testament which includes a lot which is symbolic, but inspired. Most of those writing it were not eyewitnesses.

Looking at life and the scripture people had always known, from a different perspective, is one of the main themes of the teachings of Jesus. Trying to get his contemporaries to free themselves from the mind set of "this is how we've always done it." An example is this passage from Mark.

Mark 2:18-22
18 Now John's disciples and the Pharisees were fasting; and people came and said to him, "Why do John's

disciples and the disciples of the Pharisees fast, but your disciples do not fast?" 19 Jesus said to them, "The wedding guests cannot fast while the bridegroom is with them, can they? As long as they have the bridegroom with them, they cannot fast. 20 The days will come when the bridegroom is taken away from them, and then they will fast on that day.

21 "No one sews a piece of unshrunk cloth on an old cloak; otherwise the patch pulls away from it, the new from the old, and a worse tear is made. 22 And no one puts new wine in old wineskins; otherwise, the wine will burst the skins, and the wine is lost, and so are the skins; but one puts new wine into fresh wineskins."

Jesus was there to usher in a new understanding of life, God and the scriptures. He corrected long held misconceptions and challenged his followers to think more broadly. This was not an easy task, nor was it popular among people comfortable with the box they had put God in, boundaries their limited understanding had created.

Even his followers had trouble sometimes and they were willing participants. The group who had the least trouble – the women who followed Jesus. They seemed more able to open their minds to what lay outside of the box the religious establishment had erected for God.

Chapter 3
Who Are The Inheritors?

The gospels are episodic in their depiction of the teachings and activities of Jesus. The Beatitudes are found only in the gospels of Matthew and Luke. If you read the gospels in order, they appear to be the first quoted words the bible attributes specifically to Jesus as he starts teaching the population in general.

Matthew 5:1-12:
1 When Jesus saw the crowds, he went up the

mountain; and after he sat down, his disciples came to him. 2 Then he began to speak, and taught them, saying:

3 "Blessed are the poor in spirit, for theirs is the Kingdom of Heaven."

4 "Blessed are those who mourn, for they will be comforted."

5 "Blessed are the meek, for they shall inherit the earth."

6 "Blessed are those who hunger and thirst for righteousness, for they will be filled."

7 "Blessed are the merciful, for they shall receive mercy."

8 "Blessed are the pure of heart, for they shall see God."

9 "Blessed are the peacemakers, for they will be called children of God."

10 "Blessed are those who are persecuted for righteousness' sake, for theirs is the kingdom of heaven."

11 "Blessed are you when people revile you and persecute you and utter all kinds of evil against you falsely on my account. 12 Rejoice and be glad, for your reward is great in heaven, for in the same way they persecuted the

prophets who were before you.

These first teachings, coming from a person raised in an extremely patriarchal society, do not distinguish between men and women. The Beatitudes refer to the poor, the meek, mourners without gender bias. They do not say only poor men are blessed, and who would have been considered more lowly and meek than women of that period? Women were marginalized in many ways during Jesus' day. The Beatitudes bring everyone together, giving hope to all people.

Jesus uses male and female characters in the teaching stories, or parables. There is no distinction made that any given lesson is only for one gender, and often he uses both in the same parable.

Luke 15:1-10
1 Now all the tax collectors and sinners were coming near to listen to him. 2 And the Pharisees and the scribes were grumbling and saying, "This fellow welcomes

sinners and eats with them."

3 So he told them this parable: 4 "Which one of you, having a hundred sheep and losing one of them, does not leave the ninety-nine in the wilderness and go after the one that is lost until he finds it? 5 When he has found it, he lays it on his shoulders and rejoices. 6 And when he comes home, he calls together his friends and neighbors, saying to them 'Rejoice with me, for I have found my sheep that was lost.' 7 Just so, I tell you, there will be more joy in heaven over one sinner who repents then over ninety-nine righteous persons who need no repentance.

8 "Or what woman having ten silver coins, if she loses one of them, does not light a lamp, sweep the house, and search carefully until she finds it? 9 When she has found it, she calls together her friends and neighbors, saying, 'Rejoice with me, for I have found the coin that I had lost.' 10 Just so, I tell you, there is joy in the presence of the angels of God over one sinner who repents."

Jesus could have ended the story with the male Shepard and his sheep, but instead included a female example as well. An inclusive lesson to teach men and women the importance of those who are spiritually lost, being found.

He also uses the experiences of women to illustrate the sorrow and joy the disciples will feel at his death and resurrection.

John 16:20-22

20 "Very truly, I tell you, you will weep and mourn, but the world will rejoice; you will have pain, but your pain will turn into joy. 21 When a woman is in labor, she has pain, because her hour has come. But when her child is born, she no longer remembers the anguish because of the joy of bringing a human being into the world. 22 So you have pain now; but I will see you again, and your hearts will rejoice, and no one will take your joy from you."

Birthing was not something participated in by men of Jesus time. Midwives and the pregnant woman's female relatives assisted in birth. The use of this example subtly emphasizes the equal importance of womanhood and the role women play in bringing new life into the world. As Jesus begins his ministry, clarifying the rules in scripture and performing miracles to help his people, he does so without regard to status, wealth, *or gender.*

The Pharisees and Sadducees, who were the establishment to Jesus' radical, didn't like the idea of women being included. The hierarchy of Jewish law was anything but inclusive and any alteration to that hierarchy was not something they would accept without a fight. They liked feeling superior and favored, and here comes Jesus, telling not only the downtrodden men they were equal to them and important in God's eyes, but the lowliest of lowly – the women.

Jesus shows no favoritism, not to the Pharisees, not even to his own family when someone tells him his biological family is waiting to speak to him.

Mark 3:31-35

31 Then his mother and his brothers came; and standing outside, they sent to him and called him. 32 A crowd was sitting around him; and they said to him, "Your mother and your brothers and sisters are outside, asking for you." 33 And he replied, "Who are my mother and my brothers?" 34 And looking at those who sat around him, he said, "Here are my mother and my brothers! 35 Whoever does the will of God is my brother and sister and mother."

Again, Jesus specifically includes women, referring to all who follow him and not only the male disciples. Jesus had more women than just his mother following him from town to town and he included them when he taught.

In the synagogues women were separated from the men; they were not allowed to speak and certainly not to debate scripture with the rabbi. When Jesus taught crowds of people, he did not separate the men from the women, and even children were included. Jesus showed a more egalitarian approach to teaching the Word of God. No exclusions, no divisions.

Though not specifically about women, Jesus shows his practice of inclusion in this illustration.

Mark 9:38-41

38 John said to him, "Teacher, we saw someone casting out demons in your name, and we tried to stop him, because he was not following us." 39 But Jesus said "Do not stop him; for no one who does a deed of power in my name will be able soon afterward to speak evil of me. 40 Whoever is not against us is for us. 41 For truly I tell you, whoever gives you a cup of water to drink because you bear the name of Christ will by no means lose the reward."

Notice the reversal of the oft-used phrase (especially by politicians) 'If you aren't for us, you're against us.' Instead saying, 'If you aren't against us, you are for us.' Positive reinforcement rather than negative. Reinforcement of it being okay if you weren't a recognized member of the club. Jesus wasn't about hierarchy and exclusivity, something which had grown considerably within the Jewish establishment. But that isn't how it used to be.

Back in the time of Adam and Eve, Abraham, Moses, and Noah, in the early Old Testament, God tended to go one on one with people. There was little mention of an actual church/temple hierarchy. By Jesus' time, there's a very well entrenched establishment of power and a specific chain-of-command. Jesus challenges this bureaucracy along with those in power who would prefer to keep their power. The individual responsibility for one's faith and having a personal relationship with God is, by this time, a revolutionary concept - not because it is radically new, but because the Jewish people have forgotten it.

The same thing happens to the Christian church after a few centuries. As the hierarchy of pope, cardinals, bishops, and priests becomes more established, they forget Jesus teachings of individual relationships with God. For example, when Johannes Gutenberg invents the printing press in 1440, the church at first sees the mass production of the bible as a threat. Like the Pharisees, the Catholic Church of the time had become accustomed to telling their congregations what they were supposed to believe and how they were supposed to interpret the scriptures.

Today I see a renewed interest in the idea of a personal relationship with God. The circle again curves back to the individual communion seen in the earliest biblical writings.

In Chapter 14 of Matthew, when Jesus feeds the five thousand, it's mentioned that was the number of men, and besides that there were women and children. It's significant that Jesus taught everyone without prejudice. And when Jesus talks of who will be saved in the last days, he includes women.

Matthew 24:40-41

40 "Then two will be in the field; one will be taken and one will be left. 41 Two women will be grinding meal together; one will be taken and one will be left. 42 Keep awake therefore, for you do not know on what day your Lord is coming."

Jesus repeatedly says and does things which are inclusive of all in a society which was not. Jesus further includes children, who were even lower than women in the societal hierarchy.

Mark 10:13-16

13 People were bringing little children to him in order that he might touch them; and the disciples spoke sternly to them. 14 But when Jesus saw this, he was indignant and said to them, "Let the little children come to me; do not stop them; for it is to such as these that the kingdom of God belongs. 15 Truly I tell you, whoever does not receive the kingdom of God as a little child will never enter it." 16 And he took them up in his arms, laid his hands on them and blessed them."

What an amazing message for those children to hear! "You are important to God and your faith is the example to follow." Wow! Not the pharisees and scribes and priests who told you what to think, but the children, whose faith didn't need interpretation because it was unquestioningly pure.

Miracles were another area where Jesus showed no prejudice or favoritism.

Luke 13:10-17

10 Now he was teaching in one of the synagogues on the Sabbath. 11 And just then there appeared a woman with a spirit that had crippled her for eighteen years. She was bent over and quite unable to stand up straight. 12 When Jesus saw her, he called her over and said, "Woman, you are set free from your ailment." 13 When he laid his hands on her, immediately she stood up and began praising God. 14 But the leader of the synagogue, indignant because Jesus had cured on the Sabbath, kept saying to the crowd, "There are six days on which work ought to be done; come on those days and be cured, and not on the Sabbath day." 15 But the Lord answered him and said, "You hypocrites! Does not each of you on the Sabbath untie his ox or donkey from the manger, and lead it away to give it water? 16 And ought not this woman, a daughter of Abraham whom Satan bound for eighteen long years, be set free from this bondage on the Sabbath day?" 17 When he said this, all his opponents were put to shame; and the entire crowd was rejoicing at all the wonderful things that he was doing.

I wonder if it had been a man who was cured, would this unnamed leader have been less indignant? Perhaps he would have chastised Jesus anyway. The important thing is, Jesus was showing this woman's life was more important than the rules this leader interpreted in the strictest sense. Rules which, based on what Jesus said, this leader did not follow as strictly for himself as he expected of others. He was all about exceptions made for those, like himself, who were acceptable members of the club, and thus better and more worthy than this woman. He just didn't get it.

John 3: 16

16 "For God so loved the world that he gave his only Son, so that everyone who believes in him may not perish but may have eternal life."

The world. There is no disclaimer here. It's not just the leaders of the world, or the men of the world, or the Jews or the disciples - the world. Period. Whole, as in total, all, entirely.

No exclusive club of right-thinking people were the only ones he died for. Jesus died for all people, men, women, and children. He died for those who believed in him and for those who didn't, for those who had followed him and those who killed him; he even died for those halfway around the world who would never know he existed. He died for everyone who had ever lived and everyone who was yet to be born. That is the most amazing thing possible. Who are the inheritors? We all are.

Chapter 4
Mary, the Mother of Jesus

The Gospel of Luke has always been my favorite. When I was a little girl, it was the Christmas story from Luke I wanted read because it was the most descriptive, not to mention being the one eloquently recited by Linus on *A Charlie Brown Christmas*. When you're eight years old, that's very important.

Luke is a writer's gospel, beginning with the most detailed telling of the birth of Christ. It is Luke which completely describes not only Mary's experiences with divine visitation but Elizabeth's conception of John the Baptist. More than any other gospel, Luke recognizes the stories of these women and acknowledges their contribution as important.

I refer to the women of the gospels as having a steadfast, yet quiet, faith. Jesus is shown in the gospels as testing his chosen twelve often and asking them who he is to see what they believe. But did you ever wonder about the one person who absolutely knew who and what Jesus was long before any of the rest? His mother Mary, of course. She was fully aware her son was indeed the promised Messiah and Son of God. After all, she was there when it happened, and it's not the kind of thing one forgets.

Luke 1:30-35

30 The angel said to her, "Do not be afraid, Mary, for you have found favor with God. 31 And now, you will conceive in your womb and bear a son, and you will name him Jesus. 32 He will be great, and will be called the Son of the Most High, and the Lord God will give to him the throne of his ancestor David. 33 He will reign over the house of Jacob forever, and of his kingdom there will be no end." 34 Mary said to the angel, "How can this be, since I am a virgin?" 35 The angel said to her, "The Holy Spirit will come upon you, and the power of the Most High will overshadow you; therefore the child to be born will be holy; he will be called Son of God."

So here was this quiet, ordinary young lady, newly engaged to a nice carpenter, probably thinking of the wedding celebration being planned and the new chapter in her life that was about to start. Then this angel shows up hailing her as blessed and saying her life is about to take a major detour. Shock probably doesn't even begin to cover it, and yet she had the presence of mind to ask for clarification regarding her role and how, exactly, this was supposed to happen.

Considering she knew the potential ramifications of being pregnant *before* her wedding, it would not have been surprising if she had said, "Are you sure I'm the right person for this?" No few male prophets in the Old Testament had an initial response of, "Oh no, not me." But she didn't. Like so many women in the gospels, her response was acceptance.

Luke 1:38 Then Mary said, "Here I am, the servant of the Lord; let it be with me according to your word." Then the angel departed from her.

When she visits her cousin, Elizabeth, whom she has presumably known since childhood, and who is pregnant with the future John the Baptist, she is again greeted in an extraordinary manner.

Luke 1:41-45
41 When Elizabeth heard Mary's greeting, the child leaped in her womb. And Elizabeth was filled with the Holy Spirit 42 and exclaimed in a loud cry, "Blessed are you among women, and blessed is the fruit of your womb. 43 And why has this happened to me, that the mother of my Lord comes to me? 44 For as soon as I heard the sound of your greeting, the child in my womb leaped for joy. 45

And blessed is she who believed that there would be a fulfilment of what was spoken to her by the Lord."

So here are two of the most important people in the New Testament, both women, together marveling at the rolls they have been given and accepting them at a time when "great things" were expected to be accomplished by men. They did not brag about it or even, presumably, tell their immediate friends and family. It says Mary stayed with Elizabeth for about three months, which means by the time she returned home, there would soon be no hiding her pregnancy.

This is when the Gospel of Matthew's account of Joseph comes in. His betrothed is looking less like a virgin every day, and he is likely disappointed, perhaps even heartbroken, but at the same time kind and compassionate toward her.

Matthew 1:19-25
19 Her husband Joseph, being a righteous man and unwilling to expose her to public disgrace, planned to

dismiss her quietly. 20 But just as he had resolved to do this, an angel of the Lord appeared to him in a dream and said, "Joseph, son of David, do not be afraid to take Mary as your wife, for the child conceived in her is from the Holy Spirit. 21 She will bear a son, and you are to name him Jesus, for he will save his people from their sins." 24 When Joseph awoke from sleep, he did as the angel of the Lord commanded him; he took her as his wife, 25 but had no marital relations with her until she had borne a son; and he named him Jesus.

What a revelation. The gospels do not say whether Mary tried to tell him of this before his dream, only that he did as advised. Because he went ahead and married her, and I would expect did so quickly, everyone would have assumed the child was his, saving her from public ridicule. (The Gospel of Luke seems to say they were engaged and not married until after the birth, but I find the Matthew account more likely.)

Quite a secret to be kept by them and I can just imagine some of the discussions and sense of wonder and awe they must have had, going about their daily lives as though everything was normal.

Mary accepts the most important job of any human in history with grace and humility. Even when shepherds, and then Wise Men, come to pay homage, she refrains from boasting, instead:

Luke 2:19
19 But Mary treasured all these words and pondered them in her heart.

Now, think about how proud women are of their children. I know with my three, there have been many times I wanted to shout from the rooftop "That's my son!" or "That's my daughter!" Because I have been so proud of them, so full of love for them, it just didn't seem possible to contain the feeling. And none of my children, wonderful and fabulous as they are, ever made a deaf person hear, or a blind person see, nor have they ever brought anyone back from the dead.

Jesus didn't want himself proclaimed the way

I'm sure Mary would have loved to shout from the rooftops. While she may have regaled her son's friends with stories of his childhood adventures (what mother doesn't?), I don't think she ever gave away anything which Jesus wanted to reveal at a time of his own choosing. His followers were tested frequently, yet for a long time they were left wondering. What is often forgotten is that Mary was there for all of it.

Luke 8:23-25
23 and while they were sailing, he fell asleep. A windstorm swept down on the lake, and the boat was filling with water, and they were in danger. 24 They went to him and woke him up, shouting, "Master, we are perishing!" And he woke up and rebuked the wind and the raging waves; they ceased and there was calm. 25 He said to them, "Where is your faith?" They were afraid and amazed, and said to one another, "Who then is this, that he commands even the winds and the water, and they obey him?"

Jesus' mother is mentioned as being with him in the passage immediately before this one, but as to who specifically was on the boat ... the bible only says he boarded it with his disciples and Mary was a disciple. If Mary was in the boat, I can imagine her sitting calmly with the women, a small, private smile on her face, knowing just who her son was, yet abiding by Jesus' wishes to stay quiet about it. According to Luke, at this point the men have not quite figured it out yet. (The Gospel of John differs. In John alone does Jesus state at the beginning, when they first follow him, that he is the Messiah. A fact they seem to forget regularly.)

In John we read of the wedding at Cana and the miracle of water turned to wine.

John 2:1-12

1 On the third day there was a wedding in Cana of Galilee, and the mother of Jesus was there. 2 Jesus and his disciples had also been invited to the wedding. 3 When the wine gave out, the mother of Jesus said to him, "They have no wine." 4 And Jesus said to her, "Woman, what concern is that to you and to me? My hour is not yet come." 5 His mother said to the servants, "Do whatever he tells you." 6 Now standing there were six stone water jars for the Jewish rites of purification, each holding twenty or thirty gallons. 7 Jesus said to them, "Fill the jars with water." And they filled them up to the brim. 8 He said to them, "Now draw some out and take it to the chief steward." So they took it. 9 When the steward tasted the water that had become wine, and did not know where it came from (though the servants who had drawn the water knew), the steward called the bridegroom 10 and said to him, "Everyone serves the good wine first, and then the inferior wine after the guests have become drunk. But you have kept the good wine until now." 11 Jesus did this, the first of his signs, in Cana of Galilee, and revealed his glory; and his disciples believed in him.

12 After this he went down to Capernaum with his mother, his brothers, and his disciples; and they remained there a few days.

This is one of the instances with Jesus and his mother that always makes me chuckle. The wedding in this passage likely involved a very close family member or friend. If it had been only a mild acquaintance, Mary would probably not have been as concerned about the lack of an adequate wine supply. Mary knew her son pretty well, and even though he at firsts protests, she instructs the servants to "Do whatever he tells you." She is clearly confident that her son will help out, and his help will be spectacular.

In John there is an incident in the temple which again makes me wonder if Mary was present, but silent.

John 7:40-43

40 When they heard these words, some in the crowd said, "This is really the prophet." 41 "Others said, "This is the Messiah." But some asked, "Surely the Messiah does not come from Galilee, does he? 42 Has not the scripture said that the Messiah is descended from David and comes from Bethlehem, the village where David lived?" 43 So there was a division in the crowd because of him.

Jesus could have corrected their assumption that he was born in Galilee and told them he was born in Bethlehem, but he didn't. If Mary was present at this interchange, she also apparently did not say anything about the stable in Bethlehem. Yet in the gospels this information is given, and the source of this information would logically have been his mother. After all was fulfilled and Jesus ascended, Mary would have been free to tell of the miraculous visitation of the angel, of Christ's birth and even details of his childhood she had kept to herself, although those stories never made it into the accepted bible decided upon at the Council of Nicaea. The author of Luke thought Mary's story was important, a story overlooked, or greatly abbreviated, by the other gospels.

Jesus' mother, Mary, was the one among his followers who was there before the apostles were called and who knew with certainty who and what her son was, yet she kept the information close to herself, waiting for Jesus to reveal it when he wished.

Mary is named in several passages in all four gospels as being one in the group of women following Jesus. Joseph, the human father Jesus grew up with, is not mentioned once Christ's adult ministry begins, but his mother and siblings are often mentioned. It would not have been unusual for Mary to be a widow by the time Jesus is thirty, which would explain the absence of any further mention of Mary's husband. Also, as her eldest son, it would have fallen to Jesus to care for his mother in widowhood.

Mary was warned early on of the heartbreak she would experience as the mother of the Messiah. This passage in Luke comes after the joyful birth, when Mary and Joseph present Jesus at the temple.

Luke 2: 33-35

33 And the child's father and mother were amazed at what was being said about him. 34 Then Simeon blessed them and said to his mother, Mary, "This child is destined for the falling and the rising of many in Israel, and to be a sign that will be opposed, 35 so that the inner thoughts of many will be revealed – and a sword will pierce your own soul, too."

Mary follows her son right to the end, watching him die on the cross. I cannot imagine a greater anguish for a mother than to watch her child endure such a horribly painful death.

In John, when Jesus sees his mother standing near the cross, he makes certain she will be cared for after he is gone. The often-referenced disciple referred to as the one "whom Jesus loved" is standing with her. I see this disciple as Jesus' best friend, and think that, as such, he would also have been close to Mary. If indeed Joseph is dead by this time, Jesus knows that with his passing, Mary will need a home and help. It is only John's gospel which mentions this scene.

John 19:25-27
25 Meanwhile, standing near the cross of Jesus were his mother, and his mother's sister, Mary the wife of Clopas and Mary Magdalene. 26 When Jesus saw his

mother and the disciple whom he loved standing beside her, he said to his mother, "Woman, here is your son." 27 Then he said to the disciple, "Here is your mother." And from that hour the disciple took her into his own home.

Through this final gesture to the importance of the woman who gave him birth, and the immense love he has for her, Jesus ensures she will be taken care of the rest of her mortal life.

After His resurrection, Mary continues to be part of Jesus' group of disciples. She is there at His ascension and continued with them afterward.

Acts 2:14

14 All these were constantly devoting themselves to prayer, together with certain women, including Mary the mother of Jesus, as well as his brothers.

Her witness enhances the gospels, especially Luke's, as the one person who has been there from the very beginning, with more knowledge of who and what Jesus was than anyone else.

Chapter 5
Belief and Disbelief

In many passages in the gospels, the male apostles are described as disbelieving even when events are happening right in front of them. To a certain extent, this is just human nature, especially when fear is involved. Routine, normal things are safe and predictable. When someone has difficulty accepting a bizarre concept, which could open them to an unknown they fear, they convince themselves it couldn't possibly be happening. And if you don't want to believe something is possible, it becomes easier for someone in authority to convince you that what you saw or experienced didn't really happen the way you think it did.

Take the potential existence of extra-terrestrial visitation. For some this is too scary to consider. Not to mention meaning we humans might not be on the top of the intellectual pyramid. There are people who, if they stood across the street from the White House and watched a UFO land on the front lawn, could easily be convinced it was a hoax because they do not want to believe it's possible.

The world's history shows governments have gotten away with committing atrocities because people did not wish to believe their governments capable of death camps, torture, ethnic cleansing, etc., and so were more than ready to believe the stories must have been fabricated. After all, *their* leaders would never do that. Even documented proof does not sway them. Look at the people who claim we never went to the moon or deny the holocaust happened. This is the type of mentality which allows cover ups and propaganda to be successful. Reinforce the nice, safe thing people want to believe and a large number of them will stay happily ignorant.

There were times when the apostles fell into that kind of comfort space mind-set. Take the passage in Mark where Jesus has just performed the miracle of feeding thousands with nothing more than a few loaves and fish and has sent his followers out on a boat. Keep in mind, Jesus just performed an amazing miracle.

Mark 6:47-52

47 When evening came the boat was out on the sea and he was alone on the land. 48 When he saw that they were straining at the oars against an adverse wind, he came toward them early in the morning, walking on the sea. He intended to pass them by. 49 But when they saw him walking on the sea, they thought it was a ghost and cried out; 50 for they all saw him and were terrified. But immediately he spoke to them and said, "Take heart, it is I; do not be afraid." 51 Then he got into the boat with them and the wind ceased. And they were utterly astounded, 52 for they did not understand about the loaves, but their hearts were hardened.

When the bible uses the term "hardened hearts" it seems to be describing fear or stubbornness as interfering with belief. I think "hard headed" would work, too, though it is not nearly as poetic. In the New Testament, references to hard hearts are often directed toward the male disciples or the aristocracy of the temple. In several passages Jesus seems exasperated when, even after numerous miracles, the male disciples still have trouble accepting what they have been witnessing.

The men also do not like Jesus telling them of his impending trials and death, even though he also mentions his resurrection.

Matthew 17:22-23
22 As they were gathering in Galilee, Jesus said to them, "The Son of Man is going to be betrayed into human hands, 23 and they will kill him, and on the third day he

will be raised." And they were greatly distressed.

Mark 8:31-33
31 Then he began to teach them that the Son of Man must undergo great suffering, and be rejected by the elders, the chief priests, and the scribes, and be killed, and after three days rise again. 32 He said all this quite openly. And Peter took him aside and began to rebuke him. 33 But turning and looking at his disciples, he rebuked Peter and said, "Get behind me, Satan! For you are setting your mind not on divine things but on human things."

In each passage Jesus tells not only of his death, but also of his resurrection, yet the men seem to be listening with a filter. They are so upset about the first part that they miss the last part. They don't want to believe the bad things foretold can happen to their beloved teacher. It messes with their notions of what the Messiah will do for Israel.

The women of the bible seem less inclined to this disbelief, and more accepting of the idea of letting go of preconceived notions. Perhaps this is because the changes being taught were less frightening to them. Since women of that time and place held no power, they did not stand to lose any.

In a more egalitarian doctrine, one in which the lowliest peasant was called equal to the higher caste, the Pharisees stood to lose the most political power. Face it, it doesn't matter whether it's the year 20 or the year 2020, humans who have political power and influence have difficulty letting go of it. Threaten someone's power and you get immediate back-against-the-wall resistance.

The apostles were also not immune to the desire for power and struggled with their own egos.

Mark 9:33-34

33 Then they came to Capernaum; and when he was in the house he asked them, "What were you arguing about on the way?" 34 But they were silent, for on the way they had argued with one another who was the greatest.

Luke 9:46-48

46 An argument arose among them as to which one

of them was the greatest. 47 But Jesus, aware of their inner thoughts, took a little child and put it by his side, 48 and said to them, "Whoever welcomes this child in my name welcomes me, and whoever welcomes me welcomes the one who sent me; for the least among all of you is the greatest."

The first passage is a terrific "gotcha" moment, like a teenager who realizes his or her parents just heard every word whispered on the phone about where they *really* were last night when they said they were studying. The second shows how Jesus values those on the lowest end of the social strata. Children had an even lower standing than women, and since there were children present, one can assume there were women present. How wonderful must this have sounded to them!

Women had nothing to lose, nothing to fear losing, and so much to gain from Christ's teaching. This may have been a factor in their willingness to believe. Their society was telling them they had little worth, but the Son of God told them they had value. What an incredibly powerful message for the women to hear!

Chapter 6
Heroism, or Rather, Heroine-ism

The gospels depict the women disciples as quietly heroic. They do not preach, heal, baptize, or, for the most part, openly discuss theology like the male disciples. They watch, they listen, and their quiet acts of steadfast faith speak louder than any shouted affirmation ever could.

Take, for instance, the woman in Luke who braved getting thrown out of the house of Simon the Pharisee when she came uninvited to minister to Jesus.

Luke 7:37-43

37 And a woman in the city, who was a sinner, having learned he was eating in the Pharisee's house, brought an alabaster jar of ointment. 38 She stood behind him (Jesus) at his feet, weeping, and began to bathe his feet with her tears and to dry them with her hair. Then she continued kissing his feet and anointing them with the ointment. 39 Now when the Pharisee who had invited him saw it, he said to himself, "If this man were a prophet, he would have known who and what kind of woman this is who is touching him – that she is a sinner."

40 Jesus spoke up and said to him, "Simon, I have something to say to you." "Teacher," he replied, "speak." 41 "A certain creditor had two debtors; one owed five hundred denarii, and the other fifty. 42 When they could not pay, he cancelled the debts for both of them. Now which of them will love him more?" 43 Simon answered, "I suppose the one for whom he cancelled the greater debt." And Jesus said to him, "You have judged rightly."

Simon the Pharisee was scandalized. She wasn't just a woman, she was someone seen as beneath contempt for whatever transgression she had been condemned by society for committing. Jesus then used a parable to ask Simon about the value of forgiveness, and how forgiveness of great sin will result in greater thankfulness than forgiveness of small sins. After Simon concedes to this, Jesus goes one step further to highlight how this woman Simon so looked down upon, had actually fulfilled hospitality obligations Simon himself had neglected.

Luke 7:40-48

44 Then turning to the woman, he said to Simon, "Do you see this woman? I entered your house; you gave me no water for my feet, but she has bathed my feet with her tears and dried them with her hair. 45 You gave me no kiss, but from the time I came in she has not stopped kissing my feet. 46 You did not anoint my head with oil, but she has anointed my feet with ointment. 47 Therefore, I tell you, her sins, which were many, have been forgiven; hence she has shown great love. But the one to whom little is forgiven, loves little." 48 Then he said to her, "Your sins are forgiven."

Without saying a single word this woman's actions showed a remarkable faith. Another story depicting a woman using the action of anointing Jesus to show honor and faith is told in Mark 14:3-9 (and almost identically in Matthew 26:6-13) while the disciples are gathered just before the Passover and betrayal of Jesus in Jerusalem.

Mark 14:3-9
3 While he was at Bethany in the house of Simon the leper, as he sat at table, a woman came to him with an alabaster jar of very costly ointment of nard, and she broke open the jar and she poured it on his head. 4 But some were there who said to one another in anger, "Why was the ointment wasted in this way? 5 For this ointment could have been sold for more than three hundred denarii, and the money given to the poor." 6 But Jesus said, "Let her alone; why do you trouble her? 7 She has performed a good service for me. For you always have the poor with you, and you can show kindness to them whenever you wish;

but you will not always have me. 8 She has done what she could; she has anointed my body beforehand for its burial. 9 Truly I tell you, wherever the good news is proclaimed in the whole world, what she has done will be told in remembrance of her."

The lone, unnamed female follower silently acknowledges the fate Christ is about to face, and anoints him in preparation of his death. The men, who protest every time Jesus talks of how he must die, chastise this faithful woman, who, unlike them, accepts the future Jesus faces. It makes me wonder if the women have perhaps been listening a little more attentively then the men. Her actions are an extraordinary yet simple demonstration which Jesus defends. For Jesus to tell the men to leave her alone because she is right and they are wrong must have been quite a shock for them.

The Gospel of John tells a slightly different version of this story (if it is indeed the same story, which it may not be, though the town is the same as in Mark) and names the woman anointing him as

Mary, one of the two sisters of Lazarus.

John 12:1-8

1 Six days before the Passover Jesus came to Bethany, the home of Lazarus, whom he had raised from the dead. 2 There they gave a dinner for him. Martha served, and Lazarus was one of those at the table with him. 3 Mary took a pound of costly perfume made of pure nard, anointed Jesus feet, and wiped them with her hair. The house was filled with the fragrance of the perfume. 4 But Judas Iscariot, one of his disciples (the one who would betray him), said, 5 "Why was this perfume not sold for three hundred denarii and the money given to the poor?" 6 (He said this not because he cared about the poor, but because he was a thief; he kept the common purse and used to steal what was put in it.) 7 Jesus said, "Leave her alone. She bought it so that she might keep it for the day of my burial. 8 You always have the poor, but you do not always have me."

John is the only gospel attributed to an actual Apostle of Jesus, as an eyewitness account of His teachings. It seems to me the author fills in some gaps and stories left out of the previous gospels but, as mentioned when I discussed perspective, it tells some stories quite differently. John is an interesting gospel, and only in John does Jesus state quite often and quite clearly that he is the Messiah and the Son of God. And yet even after raising Lazarus from the dead, there are still those of his own closest followers who refuse to grasp the idea.

The most profound stories of the heroic faithfulness of the women of the New Testament occur during the crucifixion and resurrection of Jesus. When Jesus is crucified it is the women, not the men, who follow to the end and watch him die. The men are depicted as scattered and panicked, shown to run away, fear for themselves, and deny knowing him.

The Gospels of Mark and Matthew, show only the women staying until the end.

Mark 15:40-41
40 There were also women looking on from a

distance; among them were Mary Magdalene, and Mary the mother of James the younger and of Joses, and Salome. 41 These used to follow him and provided for him when he was in Galilee; and there were many other women who had come up with him to Jerusalem.

>Matthew 27:55-56
>
>55 Many women were also there, looking on from a distance; they had followed Jesus from Galilee and had provided for him. 56 Among them were Mary Magdalene, and Mary the mother of James and Joseph, and the mother of the sons of Zebedee.

The Gospel of Luke gives a vague and brief grouped reference to those attending the crucifixion.

>Luke 23:49
>
>49 But all his acquaintances, including the women who had followed him from Galilee, stood at a distance.

The only specific reference to a male disciple

staying to the end comes in John 19, where Jesus tells "the disciple whom he loved" to take care of his mother. He is the only one of the men listed among the women, and in this gospel they are not described as watching at a distance, but are described as standing near the cross.

Women are the last to see Jesus as he dies, and they are the first to see him resurrected. I find this significant in an age and place where women were not seen as important, were not educated, and were largely looked at as the property of their fathers or husbands. But to Jesus, all are important. Consider the resurrection narratives of the four gospels. I'm printing all four in a row because my discussion will talk about them together.

Matthew 28:1-10

1 After the Sabbath, as the first day of the week was dawning, Mary Magdalene and the other Mary went to see the tomb. 2 And suddenly there was a great earthquake; for an angel of the Lord, descending from heaven, came and rolled back the stone and sat on it. 3

His appearance was like lightning, and his clothing white as snow. 4 For fear of him the guards shook and became like dead men. 5 But the angel said to the women, "Do not be afraid; I know that you are looking for Jesus, who was crucified. 6 He is not here; for he has been raised, as he said. Come, see the place where he lay. 7 Then go quickly and tell his disciples, 'He has been raised from the dead. And indeed he is going ahead of you to Galilee; there you will see him.' This is my message for you." 8 So they left the tomb quickly with fear and great joy, and ran to tell his disciples. 9 Suddenly Jesus met them and said, "Greetings!" And they came to him, took hold of his feet, and worshiped him. 10 Then Jesus said to them, "Do not be afraid; go and tell my brothers to go to Galilee; there they will see me."

Mark 16: 1-11

1 When the Sabbath was over, Mary Magdalene and Mary the mother of James, and Salome bought spices, so that they might go and anoint him. 2 And very early on the first day of the week, when the sun had risen, they went to the tomb. 3 They had been saying to one another, "Who will roll away the stone for us from the entrance to the tomb?" 4 When they looked up, they saw that the stone, which was very large, had already been rolled back. 5 As they entered the tomb, they saw a young man, dressed in a white robe, sitting on the right side; and they were alarmed. 6 But he said to them, "Do not be alarmed; you are looking for Jesus of Nazareth, who was crucified. He has been raised; he is not here. Look, there is the place they laid him. 7 But go, tell his disciples and Peter that he is going ahead of you to Galilee; there you will see him, just as he told you." 8 So they went out and fled from the tomb, for terror and amazement had seized them; and they said nothing to anyone, for they were afraid. 9 Now after he rose early on the first day of the week, he appeared first to Mary Magdalene, from whom he had cast out seven demons. 10 She went out and told those who had been with him, while they were mourning and weeping. 11 But when they heard that he was alive and had been seen by her, they would not believe it.

Luke 24 1-12
1 But on the first day of the week, at early dawn,

they [the women] came to the tomb, taking the spices they had prepared. 2 They found the stone rolled away from the tomb, 3 but when they went in, they did not find the body. 4 While they were perplexed about this, suddenly two men in dazzling clothes stood beside them. 5 The women were terrified and bowed their faces to the ground, but the men said to them, "Why do you look for the living among the dead? He is not here, but has risen. 6 Remember how he told you, while he was still in Galilee, 7 that the Son of Man must be handed over to sinners, and be crucified, and on the third day rise again." 8 Then they remembered his words, 9 and returning from the tomb, they told all this to the eleven and to all the rest. 10 Now it was Mary Magdalene, Joanna, Mary the mother of James, and the other women with them who told this to the apostles. 11 But these words seemed to them an idle tale, and they did not believe them. 12 But Peter got up and ran to the tomb; stooping and looking in, he saw the linen clothes by themselves; then he went home, amazed at what had happened.

John 20:1-18

1 Early on the first day of the week, while it was still dark, Mary Magdalene came to the tomb and saw the stone had been removed from the tomb. 2 So she ran and went to Simon Peter and the other disciple, the one whom Jesus loved, and said to them, "They have taken the Lord out of the tomb, and we do not know where they have laid him." 3 Then Peter and the other disciple set out and went toward the tomb. 4 The two were running together, but the other disciple outran Peter and reached the tomb first. 5 He bent down to look in and saw the linen wrappings lying there, but he did not go in. 6 Then Simon Peter came, following him, and went into the tomb. He saw the linen wrappings lying there, 7 and the cloth that had been wrapping Jesus head, not lying with the linen wrappings but rolled up in a place by itself. 8 Then the other disciple, who reached the tomb first, also went in, and he saw and believed; 9 for as yet they did not understand the scripture, that he must rise from the dead. 10 Then the disciples returned to their homes.

11 But Mary stood weeping outside the tomb. As she wept, she bent over to look in the tomb; 12 and she saw two angels in white, sitting where the body of Jesus had been lying, one at the head and the other at the feet. 13 They said to her, "Woman, why are you weeping?" She said to them "They have taken away my Lord and I do not know where they have laid him." 14 When she said this, she turned around and saw Jesus standing there, but she did not know that it was Jesus. 15 Jesus said to her, "Woman, why are you weeping? Whom are you looking for?" Supposing him to be the gardener, she said to him "Sir, if you have carried him away, tell me where you have laid him and I will take him away." 16 Jesus said to her "Mary!" She turned and said to him in Hebrew Rabbouni!" (Which means Teacher). 17 Jesus said to her, "Do not hold onto me, because I have not yet ascended to my Father. But go to my brothers and say to them 'I am ascending to my Father and your Father, to my God and your God.'" 18 Mary Magdalene went and announced to the disciples, "I have seen the Lord"; and she told them that he had said these things to her.

The Gospel of John is the longest and most descriptive resurrection narrative. In Matthew,

Mark, and John, Mary Magdalene sees Jesus before anyone else. In Luke, the women are given the first message from the angels of Christ's resurrection, but the men fail to believe the news the women proclaim. In Mark, also, they don't believe Mary. But all four gospels agree to the honor given the women and specifically, Mary Magdalene.

Jesus could have chosen anyone to be the first to see him, and he chose Mary. In the Gospel of John, the angels and Jesus are shown to actually wait until Simon Peter and "the other disciple, the one whom Jesus loved" who is referred to as male, *leave* the tomb and head home. Only once Mary is alone at the tomb do the angels and Jesus appear. Either Jesus or the angels could have appeared while Peter and his companion were still there. I wonder at the significance of this delay. Is it to further test the faith of the male apostles who, in spite of all the evidence conspicuously laid out before them, are so often called 'hard of heart'? Is it reward for the women who have been quietly steadfast throughout his ministry?

It has always seemed to me it was the women whose faith was strongest. The women who did not argue or voice doubt. In both Matthew and Mark, when Mary tells them her wonderful news, the male disciples are reluctant to believe her. They don't say if the women disciples received the news better, but I'm guessing they did. I wonder if a component in their disbelief was the fact she was a woman. Would the men have been more apt to believe one of their fellows? Perhaps the reason they do not want to believe her is jealousy, disliking the idea one of them, Jesus' hand picked chosen twelve, was not chosen for this honor. It wouldn't be the first time human ego got in the way of their faith. Could it have been one last lesson in humility?

The women who followed Jesus had unshakable faith. The men run and Peter denies knowing Christ, yet the women follow Jesus all the way to Golgotha.

I'm not saying the women were necessarily better than the men. Women were, in many ways, invisible, ignored by the priests and Romans alike.

Because of this it was perhaps safer for them to openly follow Jesus. Their belief would not have been seen as a threat to the status quo. Regardless, it is significant, and the bible does take note of their actions and how the women, who were at the bottom of the social strata, remained heroically steadfast in their faithfulness to Jesus to the end and beyond.

Chapter 7
The Gospel of Mary Magdalene

Minor references which pique my interest, or an article with something I hadn't known, often cause me to research a subject. I can't count how much history I've researched because I wanted to know what Al Stewart was referencing in a song. So it was with learning things like at one time, Catholic priests could marry, or finding out there were once many more gospels than the four in my bible.

Christianity did not start out as a separate religion. The early Christians were Jews, following the Jewish faith, who believed they'd found the Messiah. That message, shared first through an oral tradition, is what eventually became known as Christianity. In the beginning, it was not particularly well organized or structured. Instead, small groups following whichever apostle's teachings had come to them, would meet in homes to share the good news.

By the 300's there were two main groups of Christians. One group, the Gnostics, believed in a more spirit-based version of Christ's teachings with an emphasis on a personal relationship with God. The other, what was becoming the Catholic Church with its hierarchy of priests, bishops, and pope, emphasized having more learned people lead believers, who were expected to follow whatever the bishops told them. In part, it was the division of class. The educated upper class telling the lower ones what they were supposed to think and believe, with the upper class certain they truly did know better than the uneducated masses.

But even within those groups there were

differing opinions and schools of thought, which caused arguments and divisiveness. A pivotal event was when the Emperor Constantine of Rome converted to and legalized Christianity, along with all religions in Rome. This officially ended persecution of religions by the Roman Empire.

As Emperor, Constantine was often asked to act as judge in religious disputes between schools of belief. This sparked the eventual convening of the First Council of Nicaea, and subsequent councils over many years. The goal was to establish a single doctrine everyone would follow, rather than the multiple sects who sometimes argued violently with each other over who's interpretation of Christ's teaching's was correct. Constantine wanted an orderly consensus. It's not surprising, as Romans really liked organization. (They may have invented bureaucracy, for which I'm not sure we should revere or curse them.)

In 325 A.D. Constantine brought church leaders together to decide what would be the uniform Christian doctrine and to devise a single creed. Among the discussions was whether Jesus was human or divine. It was the beginning of what evolved into the Roman Catholic Church. Over the years, subsequent councils decided which of the many gospels would be considered proper and which would be omitted and condemned as heresy.

All the Gnostic gospels were eliminated. Not surprising considering their stress on individual spirituality was in opposition to the idea of a human church hierarchy. The authority figures of the developing formal church would likely have felt their influence threatened by such ideas. Though I am certain they truly believed themselves to be in the right, it seems yet another example of how those in power, or in the process of acquiring power, do not willingly relinquish it.

The Gnostics concentrated on a more mystical approach to belief and looking within oneself to have a close personal relationship with the divine. They also did not limit women's participation or leadership. This contradicted Roman society, which did not give women equal status to men. So a gospel written from a woman's perspective, even one as important as Mary Magdalene, would not have been welcome. The Council of Laodicea in 352 C.E. further limited women's power within the church, espousing that women were created to be subservient to men.

Consider that in the midst of all this, by the end of that century Bishop Augustine, who would later be St. Augustine – one of the most important figures in the early Catholic Church – refers to Mary Magdalene as "the Apostle to the Apostles." He acknowledged her having been with Jesus all the way to the cross, and she is the one Jesus first reveals himself to after the resurrection. How conflicted might those early church leaders have felt, treating women in general as unimportant, yet having to acknowledge that this woman was very important to Christ.

How different might Christianity be if all the gospels had been included? The early church saw Gnostic gospels as contradictory to the four gospels which became accepted. No attempt seems to have been made to blend the different ways the two groups saw spirituality and Jesus' teachings and I think they especially did not want a gospel written from a woman's perspective. There were no women on Constantine's council. The male dominated Roman society of the time, including the church, saw the Gnostic's practice of including women as scandalous. Sadly, this otherwise forward thinking, representative government did not represent half its population very well. I wonder if there was a Roman women's suffrage movement?

Of course, the first thing to impress me in all this, was learning there once was a written Gospel of Mary Magdalene. How awesome! I hope someday archeologists will find a complete version of her gospel. It would be fascinating to read. It is amazing and wonderful to learn there were sects of early Christianity which included women and took what they said seriously. It took the newly codified church nearly two thousand years to take women even marginally seriously and if it weren't for Martin Luther's reformation, there might still be no female pastors. Luther, while I doubt he thought women were equal since he was quoted as saying they should look after the household only, did begin the branch of Christianity (protestant, not specifically Lutheran) which eventually saw the first women pastors ordained.

Recently I was pleased to learn there are female Catholic priests in the United States. They are not recognized by Rome, and many have been technically excommunicated, but they are priests and minister faithfully to the home churches who accept them. They see the calling from God as more important than the box of rules and confines man has made. Was Mary Magdalene the first woman priest? She was an apostle by any definition you can give which does not include gender, and she is now commonly referred to as "the Apostle to the Apostles."

Biblical scholars have debunked the long-held misconception of Mary Magdalene being a reformed prostitute. These views regarding Mary Magdalene can be traced to Pope Gregory I, in the late 6th Century, when his homily combined three separate women from the gospels (Mary Magdalene, Mary of Bethany and an anonymous "sinful woman" from Luke 7:37) into one: Mary Magdalene.

"She whom Luke calls the sinful woman," said Pope Gregory I, "whom John calls Mary, we believe to be the Mary from whom seven devils were ejected according to Mark. What did these seven devils signify, if not all the vices?"

Seriously? I can think of all kinds of things they could have signified, including epilepsy, schizophrenia, bi-polar disorder, Tourette syndrome - and that's just a few. After reading all three passages, it is clear to me they are three different people, Mary being a very popular name in Jesus's time. (Kind of like how my son, Matthew, often had three or four other Matthews in his class every year.) The negative picture he painted of her unfortunately stuck for a long time. He also gave the impression of Mary as young and seductive. In truth we have no idea how old she was, but it is not inconceivable she was in her forties or fifties.

Gregory I, whose term was 590-604, was also the pope who declared all sexual desire was inherently sinful. This was part of an ongoing argument on the practice of clergy marrying. By this time there had been a steady devolution of the participation of women in the church and a split personality regarding women and sex was developing.

In Jewish tradition, sex within marriage is considered a blessing, something joyful and fulfilling, not to mention the one sure way to have babies. Peter and the disciples were likely all married. It would have been extremely unusual if they hadn't been. But even St. Augustine, who had so progressively referred to Mary Magdalene as "the Apostle to the Apostles" also said, "Nothing is so powerful in drawing the spirit of a man downwards as the caresses of a woman." This is part of the ridiculous notion that men cannot control themselves around women, a belief which has been used for centuries to justify rape and even the wholesale blaming of Eve for original sin. Were I a man, I would find this idea insulting.

So poor Mary Magdalene became the embodiment and scapegoat for all the perceived evils of the flesh. Yet the bible clearly shows Mary as a disciple of Jesus and important to him. Today it is generally accepted Mary Magdalene was wealthy, a rare independent woman, perhaps a childless widow, and among the financial backers of Christ's ministry.

Luke 8:1-3

1 Soon afterwards he went on through cities and villages, proclaiming and bringing the good news of the kingdom of God. The twelve were with him, 2 as well as some women who were cured of evil spirits and infirmities; Mary, called Magdalene, from whom seven demons had gone out, 3 Joanna, the wife of Herod's steward Chuza, and Suzanna, and many others, who provided for them out of their resources.

It was the women who apparently earned the

money the men needed for Christ's ministry. After all, even Apostles have to eat. And these women learned the lessons Jesus taught right alongside the men. Could there be Gospels of Joanna? Or of Suzanna? Or of Martha and Mary? Or even his mother, Mary? The women who were among his closest followers would not have remained silent about what they learned from him.

Was Jesus trying to bring back the idea of women as partners, equal to men? He certainly seemed to be planting the seeds of it. And keeping in mind the "big picture" regarding cosmically figured time, the two thousand years since Jesus walked the earth is the blink of an eye for God.

2 Peter 3:8

8 But do not ignore this one fact, beloved, that with the Lord one day is like a thousand years, and a thousand years are like one day.

It was a male dominated society in Jesus' time. And while the gospels show Jesus valued women equally to men, some of his contemporaries had a harder time grasping the concept. The church which eventually grew out of the movement, started by Christ and spread by his followers both male and female, eventually succumbed to the view of the more biased leaders, and women were steadily pushed back to second-class status for centuries.

Thankfully much of society has evolved to accept, if not yet a truly egalitarian model, one that is much closer than it ever has been since Jesus' time. If Mary Magdalene's gospel had been included in the accepted books of the bible, perhaps it wouldn't have taken the better part of two thousand years to accomplish this.

Chapter 8
Marriage, Divorce and Adultery

For the purpose of this chapter, I will talk only about heterosexual, monogamous marriage. Why? Because as I read it, that's what Jesus was being asked about – the state of marriage in Israel at that time and the practice of easy divorces. I personally believe every type of marriage, if all parties involved are willing participants who love and respect one another, can be blessed by God, for God loves all of us and wants us to also be loved.

****

Marriage was important in Jesus' time and still is today. I think it significant Jesus' first recorded miracle was at a wedding, the joyous event when two people join their hearts, lives, and families together, celebrating the couple's public commitment to care and support one another through all life's trials.

The teachings of Jesus regarding marriage and adultery are in all four gospels. The Jews of the time followed a law Moses had created saying a man may divorce his wife by simply giving her a paper "certificate of divorce" and sending her out of his house. His only reason needed to be that he "found something objectionable" about her. How arbitrary. And the law seemed to give the power of divorce only to the man. How many women lived in fear their husbands might do this to them, knowing they would have no recourse?

When Jesus teaches about adultery and divorce he brings more balance. Jewish law at the time mostly benefitted the man. Adultery was blamed on the woman, and she could be stoned for it. But Jesus makes adultery a gender neutral sin, not just a female one. Take this incident in the Gospel of John.

John 8:3-11
3 The scribes and the Pharisees brought a woman who had been caught in adultery; and making her stand before all of them, 4 they said to him, "Teacher, this woman was caught in the very act of committing adultery. 5 Now in the law, Moses commanded us to stone such women. Now what do you say?" 6 They said this to test him, so that they might have some charge to bring against him. Jesus bent and wrote with his finger on the ground. 7 When they kept on questioning him, he straightened up and said to them, "Let anyone among you who is without sin be the first to throw a stone at her." 8 And once again he bent down and wrote on the ground.

There's an asterisk and interesting notation in my bible that says, "Other ancient authorities add the sins of each of them" was what Jesus was writing in the dirt. How nervous might that have made her accusers? Especially if the guilty man's name was one of the things written.

> 9 When they heard it, they went away, one by one, beginning with the elder; and Jesus was left alone with the woman standing before him. 10 Jesus straightened up and said to her, "Woman, where are they? Has no one condemned you?" 11 She said, "No one, sir." And Jesus said, "Neither do I condemn you. Go your way, and from now on do not sin again."

Whenever I hear this gospel passage in church, my first thought is always: "So where is the man who was committing adultery with her?" By this time adultery has somehow morphed into an offense only the woman would be punished for, yet this was not the original law Moses gave them.

> *Deuteronomy 22:22*
> 22 If a man is caught lying with the wife of another man, both of them shall die, the man who lay with the woman as well as the woman.

Apparently by Jesus' time they completely forgot about stoning the man. Jesus not only uses this lesson to show they had no right to judge her, since they were also not perfect, but refuses to punish only her for something two people were guilty of. Instead, he forgives her.

In Matthew, Jesus also addresses the desire to cheat, and how one can betray their spouse even before committing the physical act.

Matthew 5:27-28

27 "You have heard that is was said, 'You shall not commit adultery.' 28 But I say to you that everyone who looks at a woman with lust has already committed adultery with her in his heart."

In this passage, there are a couple of things which would have shocked those hearing it. First, Jesus refers to the man as the guilty one. Second, it can be argued that he is also telling men it's wrong to objectify women.

In Matthew 5:31, Jesus goes on to correct the

law where a man could divorce his wife, leaving her penniless and destitute, simply by giving her a certificate of divorce for no more reason than she "displeased" him, giving men the legal right to be fickle and giving women no protection.

Matthew 19:9
9 "whoever divorces his wife, except for unchastity, and marries another, commits adultery."

He further says Moses allowed and tolerated the practice, but that it was never what God intended.

Matthew 19:8
8 He said to them, "It was because you were so hard-hearted that Moses allowed you to divorce your wives, but from the beginning it was not so."

In this passage he is addressing the men of Israel, and telling them they were wrong to begin the practice of such easy and arbitrary divorces.

The message being that marriage is a blessed *commitment*, and when things start to go wrong, a couple needs to look to each other, and to faith, not to an extramarital relationship.

However, the following passage has caused my feminist views and my spiritual beliefs to have no few battles.

Matthew 5:31
31 "It was also said, Whoever divorces his wife, let him give her a certificate of divorce.' 32 But I say to you that anyone who divorces his wife, except on the grounds of unchastity, causes her to commit adultery."

This can be a troubling passage in this day of 50% divorce rates. I struggled with it enormously after my first husband of twenty-five years committed adultery and then abandoned me. I remained faithful, even during the two-and-a-half-year separation before the divorce was final. Separation is not divorce; I saw myself as still married and bound by my vows, even though everyone I knew secularly disagreed. I discussed with my pastor what this passage means for the person who is the victim of faithlessness and subsequently is left behind by the partner who commits adultery. I wondered if I must remain faithful to him, even though divorced, to keep from committing adultery myself, which is a very harsh prospect. But the one valid reason Jesus gave was unchastity. The definition of unchastity is "not virtuous" which, by committing adultery, my first husband certainly wasn't. According to these teachings, this meant my divorce from him was for the right reason, while his divorce from me was not.

It was another two years after the divorce finalized, before the issue came up for me in more than a theoretical sense. A miracle happened (at least, as far as I am concerned it was a miracle) when I found myself feeling romantic love for a wonderful man, a widower, who was a dear and close friend. Happily, the feelings were reciprocated and I felt free to honestly pledge myself to someone more worthy.

Now, I certainly don't believe Jesus meant for a woman to stay with a man who brutalizes and abuses her. A man who abuses his wife is certainly not virtuous. Rather I see Jesus as more specifically addressing the arbitrary way a husband of his time could dismiss his wife. A practice the scribes and Pharisees were asking him to validate.

In Luke, when listing some of the commandments, adultery is the first he details when talking to the Pharisee who asks how he can inherit eternal life.

Luke 18:20

20 "You know the commandments: You shall not commit adultery; you shall not murder; you shall not steal; you shall not bear false witness; Honor your father and mother."

Jesus lists adultery first, even though you shall not murder is the sixth commandment and you shall not commit adultery is the seventh. Honor your father and mother is the fifth commandment, but is listed here last. Am I reading too much into the order Jesus lists these commandments to this man? Possibly. Or maybe Jesus knew this particular man was contemplating adultery, and so he emphasized it. I also wonder whether the divorce rate, and the sin of adultery, were perhaps happening far too frequently during Jesus' time, and so he stressed it as a reminder.

In all these passages Jesus makes one thing abundantly clear - adultery is wrong. Period. There are no exceptions given, no escape clauses, no acceptable excuses. When you marry someone and promise to be faithful, you're expected to keep your promise, or you shouldn't be making the vow in the first place.

The temptation to commit adultery is opportunistic and has many faces. Here are just a few examples.

At mid-life one spouse feels disappointed their life hasn't gone the way they imagined it would. They start second guessing their choices, including their choice of life mate. Temptation makes it easy to blame the other spouse for everything they see as missed opportunities. In their mind they may begin to rewrite their personal history to match this perception and justify their affair to themselves.

Maybe the tempted spouse is young, inexperienced, and has had a terribly painful argument. This spouse begins to fear getting married was a mistake. Marriage was supposed to be as easy as the love songs and movies promise, but reality is far more complicated.

Sometimes the temptation comes while one spouse is away: too many business trips, or military service causing long and lonely separations. Temptation may also come during the exhausting battle with a spouse's grave illness or injury.

Temptation will arrive, for whatever reason, when we are weakest. It is a test which a spouse can pass by refusing to act on the temptation. It is a test a spouse can fail, if he or she succumbs to the temptation. Regardless of the reasons, acting on it means failing the test. The betrayal of adultery can never be excused, only forgiven.

Spouses who feel disconnected and unhappy in their marriages need to remember they have resources available to them. Marriage counseling, clergy, encounter groups, even just sitting down with your spouse for an honest conversation about what you are feeling. All of these, even the conversation, takes courage and commitment to the vows each took when they got married. It means facing what could turn into a very unpleasant confrontation, possibly hearing some truths about themselves they don't want to hear. Often the courage needed for this is in short supply.

Feeling the temptation to stray should be a red flagged alarm that something is terribly wrong and needs to be addressed in the marriage. Succumbing looks and feels like the easy way out, as running away from one's problems often does. It takes less work and much less courage to run than it does to stay and fight for your marriage. As the tempted spouse looks at the attractive lure of the false light of an affair, the repercussions and painful consequences are hidden in the shadows cast by this enticing false light.

I readily admit the damage caused by adultery is rather keen in my psyche. The wounds of such a betrayal are deep and can last a lifetime. I was very happily remarried and yet I still struggled at times with the scars left by my ex-husband's betrayal. My second husband, Bari, was helping me cope with them and heal. With Bari's death, my grief has threatened to break the scars open again, so it is still a battle I consciously wage years later.

Jesus wanted spouses to be respectful of each other and take their marriage seriously, not see it as a commitment of convenience to be tossed aside the moment life becomes difficult. When a spouse commits adultery, he or she hurts themselves, their spouse, their children, their own family, their spouse's family, and their friends – the devastating ripples keep spreading and multiplying exponentially. It is no wonder Jesus wanted to see his people work on their relationships, respect each other, and stop committing adultery.

Chapter 9
Was Jesus Married?

It's the religious sixty-four thousand dollar question: Was Jesus married? I am fascinated by this subject. I wonder at those who staunchly insist it is totally beyond the realm of consideration. My question for them is: "Why not?"

No, I'm not purporting the more radical notion of those who claim Mary Magdalene was his wife. Rather, I think it more plausible that he was married during the nearly twenty years where the bible is silent on his whereabouts, between age twelve and age thirty. More believable to me is the prospect he is a widower when he begins his ministry.

Why? Think about the reason Jesus came to earth in the first place. To be one of us, to experience what we experience. God as human.

John 1:14
14 And the Word became flesh and lived among us, and we have seen his glory, the glory as of a father's only son, full of grace and truth.

Hebrews 2:14
14 Since, therefore, the children share flesh and blood, he himself likewise shared the same things, so that through death he might destroy the one who has the power of death, that is, the devil, 15 and free those who all their lives were held in slavery by the fear of death.

God didn't send us an angel or an intangible spirit. He sent his human son, conceived in a human woman, to be human. It's wonderful to think our loving God, who sent part of himself to earth to experience the whole of what it means to be human, might have also experienced the joy of romantic love and the fulfillment of that love through marriage. This is the essence of what it means to be human, to bond with another human on an emotional, spiritual and physical level. To become "one flesh" as God intended.

I like to think Jesus spent the years before his ministry discovering all that it is to be human. That would include finding a woman with whom to share love and have a partnership. Then, to understand the depth of our sorrows, that he might also have experienced the grief of losing the wife he loved.

I also think it quite believable Jesus could have had a child. And no, much as I enjoyed *The DaVinci Code* I do not think there is a descendant out there somewhere. I just believe that it is possible Jesus married and had a child and then both died.

Radical idea? Why? Having and losing both wife and child would mean Jesus experiencing the greatest joy, and also the most horrendous grief, humanly possible.

My second husband was the most wonderful man I ever met. He was my soul mate, my true partner in love and life. He was indeed the other half of me. Losing him to a heart attack at fifty was devastatingly painful. The depth of my grief was greater than anything I had ever experienced. And yet I can tell you, as the mother of three, I know even that pain would pale in comparison to losing one of my precious children. With two grown and one still at home, there is no worse horror I can imagine.

If Jesus was married, and lost his wife in childbirth (not a rare instance, certainly), or sometime after lost both wife and child to illness or accident, it would mean Jesus was willing to endure not only the worst physical pain through his crucifixion, but the worst emotional pain by having those he loves ripped away from him. It is the kind of grief which causes no few people to doubt their belief in God. Would not that have completed Jesus experiencing all of what it means to be human?

I do not understand why some bristle so much at the notion of a married Jesus. How does Jesus being married diminish the message of his teaching? It doesn't. Nor does it negate that he was the only Son of the Living God. He was also human. Wasn't that the point?

I think for some it is the idea of Jesus having sexual intercourse which is most disconcerting, the lingering effects of a societal view that sex is somehow dirty. Pure, perfect Jesus can't be seen as participating in carnal desire. They forget it isn't the act but the intent behind it which determines morality. Even the Puritans, so often represented as prudish, encouraged enjoyment of sex as long as you were married. Sex is part of what it is to be human. God made humanity capable of pleasure in the joining of one body to another, separating us from animals procreating out of instinct alone. A dog in heat cannot chose to abstain. (And after witnessing dog copulation, I don't think it was pleasant for either of them.) It is different for an aroused human, who not only experiences pleasure, but can abstain, or participate by their choice, not forced by instinct.

God became human through Jesus to experience all of what it means to be lowly, mortal us, then to sacrifice himself to gain forgiveness of all our sins, past, present, and future. The concept of Jesus being married does nothing to change or diminish what he taught and accomplished. In fact, for me, the idea actually enhances it by showing he was willing to truly experience all it meant to be human, not just select things.

Chapter 10
The Role of Women in Ministry

There is a wonderful story in the Gospel of John where Jesus brings both an egalitarian view to people, while tearing down long-held prejudices against Samaritans. The Samaritans were Jews, descended from the same tribes as those in Jerusalem. A schism that occurred generations previous had left them apart and frowned upon by the Jews of Jerusalem. But Jesus illustrates God's desire for all his children to get along and accept one another.

In John 4:5-30, he carries on a theological discussion with someone seen as having two strikes against her: she was a woman and also a Samaritan. Just how extraordinary an event this was is hard to understand by today's sensibilities. Back then, a woman expressing to a Rabbi an opinion on the Jewish faith was nearly unheard of. Women weren't even supposed to talk to men unless related to them. This woman has chutzpah, I like that. The example I see Jesus setting is that a woman with a brain should not be afraid to use her God-given intellect.

John 4:5-30

5 So he came to a Samaritan city called Sychar, near the plot of ground Jacob had given to his son Joseph. 6 Jacob's well was there, and Jesus, tired out from his journey, was sitting by the well. It was about noon.

7 A Samaritan woman came to draw water, and Jesus said to her "Give me a drink." 8 (His disciples had gone to the city to buy food.) 9 The Samaritan woman said to him, "How is it that you, a Jew, ask a drink of me, a woman of Samaria?" (Jews do not share things in common with Samaritans.) 10 Jesus answered her, "If you knew the gift of God, and who it is that is saying to you, 'Give me a drink,' you would have asked him, and he would have given you living water." 11 The woman said to him, "Sir, you have no bucket, and the well is deep. Where do you get that living water? 12 Are you greater than our ancestor Jacob, who gave us the well, and with his sons and his flocks drank from it?" 13 Jesus said to her, "Everyone who drinks from this water will be thirsty again, 14 but those who drink from the water that I will give them will never be thirsty. The water that I will give will become in them a spring of water gushing up to eternal life." 15 The woman said to him, "Sir, give me this water, so I may never be thirsty or have to keep coming here to draw water."

16 Jesus said to her, "Go, call your husband, and come back." 17 The woman answered him, "I have no husband." Jesus said to her, "You are right in saying, 'I have no husband'; 18 for you have had five husbands, and the one you have now is not your husband. What you have said is true!" 19 The woman said to him, "Sir, I see that you are a prophet. 20 Our ancestors worshiped on this mountain, but you say the place where people must worship is in Jerusalem." 21 Jesus said to her, "Woman, believe me, the hour is coming when you will worship neither on this mountain nor in Jerusalem. 22 You worship what you do not know; we worship what we know, for salvation is from the Jews. 23 But the hour is coming, and is now here, when the true worshipers will worship the Father in spirit and truth, for the Father seeks such as these to worship him. 24 God is spirit, and those who worship him must worship in spirit and truth." 25 The woman said to him, "I know the Messiah is coming" (who is called Christ). "When he comes he will proclaim all things to us." 26 Jesus said to her, "I am he, the one who is speaking to you."

27 Just then the disciples came. They were astonished that he was speaking with a woman, but no one said, "What do you want?" or "Why are you speaking with her?" 28 Then the woman left her water jar and went back to the city. She said to the people, 29 "Come and see a man who told me everything I have ever done! He cannot be the Messiah, can he?" 30 They left the city and were on their way to him.

The text does not mention details of the woman's circumstances. Has she been widowed five times? Or has she been the victim of five men who abandoned her, handing her a "certificate of divorce" and tossing her out on the street? The text implies she's considered a woman of ill repute, a reputation which may, or may not, be one she deserves. It only says that she is currently living with a man to whom she is not married. Yet she does not flinch when he asks about her husband, she merely states fact. Perhaps she is just doing what she must to survive in a time when women alone were at an extreme disadvantage unless they were wealthy. I can imagine her burned out by the pain and grief of losing, or being left by, five men who must have, at some point, claimed to love her. Perhaps she loves the man she is with and is forced to accept his terms. Even today, how many women stay in abusive or unhappy relationships because they either love the person and think he will change, or because their tormentor has convinced them they deserve no better. We don't know the details of her circumstances, but Jesus *does*, and he chooses to speak with her in a compassionate manor which also respects her intelligence.

This woman then goes off to the city and testifies about Jesus, becoming a disciple in her own right. First, he revealed himself as the Messiah to her. Then she went out and testified on his behalf. Continued here:

John 4:39-42

39 Many Samaritans from that city believed in him because of the woman's testimony, "He told me everything I have ever done." 40 So when the Samaritans came to him, they asked him to stay with them; and he stayed there two days. 41 And many more believed because of his word. 42 They said to the woman, "It is no longer because of what you said that we believe, for we have heard for ourselves, and we know that this is truly the Savior of the world."

Jesus leaves the city then, and I have to wonder about the woman. Did she continue to spread the word of Jesus? Did she help found a congregation there? Not all of Jesus' followers physically went with him. He left followers everywhere he preached. Many of the early churches, simple gatherings of believers in private homes, were led by women. In no few of the Letters of Paul, he addresses "sisters in Christ" as well as brothers, acknowledging women as fellow disciples spreading the teachings of Christ.

The story of Martha and Mary is another which shatters the cultural taboos of the time regarding the teaching of women and the appreciation of a woman's intellect.

Luke 10:38-42

38 Now as they went on their way, he entered a certain village, where a woman named Martha welcomed him into her home. 39 She had a sister named Mary, who sat at the Lord's feet and listened to what he was saying. 40 But Martha was distracted by her many tasks; so she came to him and asked, "Lord, do you not care that my sister has left me to do all the work by myself? Tell her then to help me." 41 But the Lord answered her, "Martha, Martha, you are worried and distracted by many things; 42 there is need of only one thing. Mary has chosen the better part, which will not be taken away from her."

I love this message: intellect and learning are more important than housework! Jesus emphasized the importance of scholarship, and the value of teaching the understanding of scripture to everyone. In an age when women were not allowed to be scholars (there were no women Pharisees or Scribes), Jesus openly recognized women were intelligent and insightful.

In John, from chapters 15 through 17, Jesus gives his disciples extensive instructions regarding what to do after he is gone, concluding in Chapter 17 with a prayer for them.

John 17:6-11
6 "I have made your name known to those whom

you gave me from this world. They were yours, and you gave them to me, and they have kept your word. 7 Now they know that everything you have given me is from you; 8 for the words that you gave to me I have given to them, and they have received them and know in truth that I came from you; and they have believed that you sent me. 9 I am asking on their behalf; I am not asking on behalf of the world, but on behalf of those you gave to me, because they are yours. 10 All mine are yours, and yours are mine; and I have been glorified in them. 11 And now I am no longer in the world, but they are in the world and I am coming to you. Holy Father, protect them in your name that you have given me, so that they may be one, as we are one.

The prayer continues, and at no point does it say he is talking to or about only the twelve, but to the entire faithful core group who had been following him. This included many women, and so they, too, were being given the instructions and being prayed for. In other passages, it's also very clear there are more than twelve spreading Jesus teachings.

Luke 10:1-11

1 After this the Lord appointed seventy others and sent them on ahead in pairs to every town and place where he himself intended to go. 2 He said to them, "The harvest is plentiful, but the laborers are few; therefore ask the Lord of the harvest to send out laborers into his harvest. 3 Go on your way. See, I am sending you out like lambs into the midst of wolves. 4 Carry no purse, no bag, no sandals; and greet no one on the road. 5 Whatever house you enter, first say, 'Peace to this house!' 6 And if anyone is there who shares in peace, your peace will rest on that person; but if not, it will return to you. 7 Remain in the same house, eating and drinking whatever they provide, for the laborer deserves to be paid. Do not move about from house to house. 8 Whenever you enter a town and its people welcome you, eat what is set before you; 9 cure the sick who are there and say to them, 'The kingdom of God has come near you.' 10 But whenever you enter a town and they do not welcome you, go out into its streets and say, 11 'Even the dust of your town that clings to our feet, we wipe off in protest against you. Yet know this: the kingdom of God has come near."

Though not specified, some of these seventy could easily have been married couples, or brother-sister pairs. Clearly not only the twelve chosen are sent. In fact, if only the twelve had been allowed to spread Jesus' message, Christianity would be a small religious sect instead of the largest religion in the world with 2.1 billion followers.

Remember the old shampoo commercial where the model says she told two friends and they told two friends and so on? (Okay, fine, nobody under the age of forty is going to remember that one.) The idea being, if you tell a couple of people about something, you start a conversation about it which continues and is passed along to others. This was Christianity's beginning. Men and women going out to share the good news. News that we are all valuable no matter where on the societal ladder we stand; that we are loved unconditionally, no matter how poor or sick; that we are important to

God, and his son died to forgive our sins, regardless of our gender. Everyone, all inclusive, no clubs, no pedigree tests, no proof of residency. If you're human, you're in.

And look what those humble beginnings have become. Not perfect, for no human construct can ever be perfect. Christianity has certainly had its struggles, missteps, and spectacular stumbles. People have wrongly done horrific things in the name of Christianity. Still, as a whole, it gets up, shakes off the dust, and usually tries to learn from the experience and do better next time. Like not arresting people for saying the Earth travels around the sun.

I hope Christianity continues to reach, to evolve, to learn from mistakes of the past and to grow closer to the loving, inclusive spirituality Jesus taught. We can never be perfect, but it shouldn't stop us from trying. It is the striving that's important, continuing to try to be better than we are, individually and as a whole.

This book is my way of starting a discussion,

an inclusive one. So look at this as my way of telling two people, like the old shampoo commercial, in the hope it will start a conversation. Thanks for listening.

About the Author

Ms. Greenberg is a writer and singer-songwriter originally from southern Illinois who now calls St. Louis, Missouri home where she lives with cats, a dog and a toddler, so life is never boring. She is the owner of Mountain Cat Media LLC, opened with her late husband, Bari, in 2012 and writes the blog *An Ordinary Feminist* at mountaincatmedia.com. While this is her first non-fiction work, she has been writing fiction on and off for nearly 30 years and spent 14 years as the advertising director for *The Bulletin of the Science Fiction and Fantasy Writers of America*.

www.ingramcontent.com/pod-product-compliance
Lightning Source LLC
Chambersburg PA
CBHW071514040426
42444CB00008B/1638